Read and Do

QUIET AND LOUD

Doug Kincaid and Peter Coles

Library of Congress Cataloging in Publication Data

Kincaid, Doug, 1940-
Quiet and loud.

(Read and do)
Summary: Text and photographs explain through observation and simple experiments how sound travels, what things are loud, what things are quiet, and different kinds of sounds.
1. Sound—Juvenile literature. [1. Sound. 2. Noise] I. Coles, Peter, 1954- . II. Title. III. Series: Kincaid, Doug, 1940- . Read and do.
QC225.5.K49 1984 534 84-12714
ISBN 0-86625-234-7

Rourke Publications, Inc.
Vero Beach, FL 32964

Read

Sometimes it is quiet.

Sometimes there are loud sounds.

Playtime is a loud time.

Bedtime is a quiet time.

The library is a quiet place.

The fairground is a loud place.

Look at the pictures.

Some things make a loud sound.

Name them.

Some things make a quiet sound.

Name them.

and Do

Read

A tape recorder can record sounds.
It can record loud sounds.
It can record quiet sounds.
A needle can show how loud.
It can show how quiet.

Use a tape recorder.

Record loud sounds.

Record quiet sounds.

Play the tape to a friend.

Which were the loud sounds?

Which were the quiet sounds?

and Do

Read

The radio can be loud.

The radio can be quiet.

This knob can be turned.

It can make the sound loud.

It can make the sound quiet.

Use a radio.

Turn the knob.

Make the sound loud.

Make the sound quiet.

Move away.

How far away can you hear each sound?

and Do

Read

These things were dropped.

The letter made a quiet sound.

The pan made a loud sound.

The plate made a loud sound.

The glove made a quiet sound.

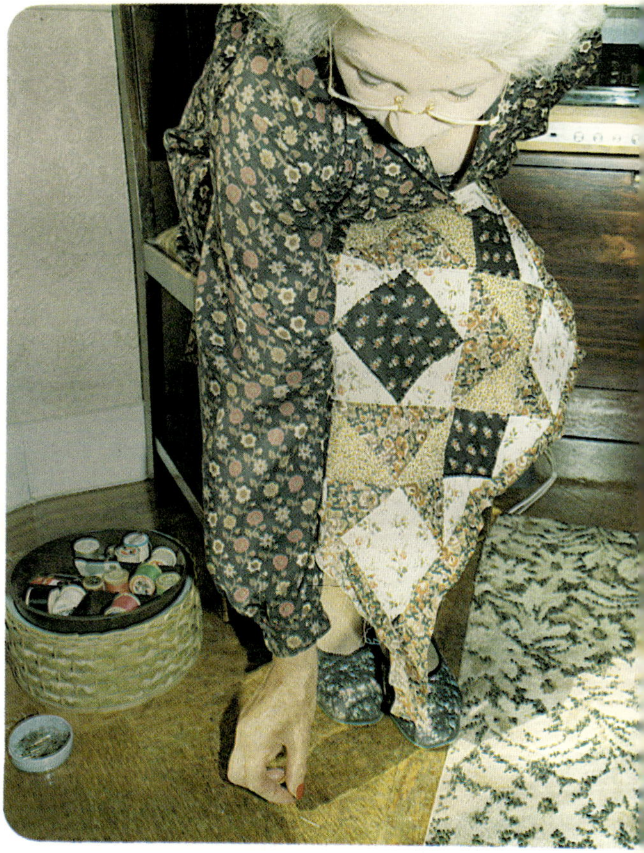

The pin made a quiet sound.

Can you hear a pin drop?
Listen to find out.
How far away can you hear it?
Make the test fair.
Move fifteen feet away.
Move till you cannot hear it drop.

and Do

Read

These made loud sounds.

The tin made a clang.

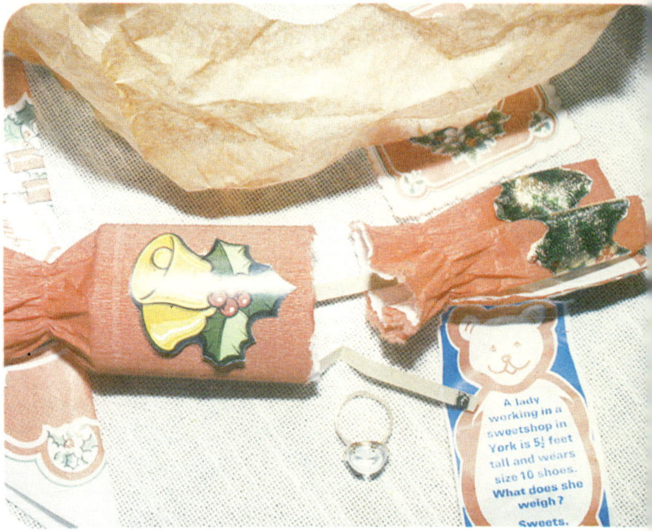

The cracker made a bang.

The box made a clatter.

A carpet can make some sounds qui

Drop a coin on the table.
Drop a coin on the floor.
Drop a coin on the carpet.
Drop a coin on the grass.
Drop a coin on the path.
Name the loud sounds.
Name the quiet sounds.
Put them in order.

and Do

Read

This car is far away.

The sound is quiet.

The car is now near.

The sound is loud.

The car is going away.

The sound is quiet.

Listen to keep safe.

Make marks on the ground.
Make a quiet sound.
Make it at different marks.
Listen to the sound.
Say how far away it is.

and Do

Read

The coat has a hood.

It can keep you warm.

It can keep you dry.

It can cover your ears.

Can you hear as well?

Is there a danger?

Try a test.
Do this with a friend.
Make a quiet sound.
Listen with the hood down.
Listen with the hood up.
Can you hear as well?

and Do

Read

Some sounds are quiet.
We need to make them loud.
Here are some things that can help.
They make sounds loud.

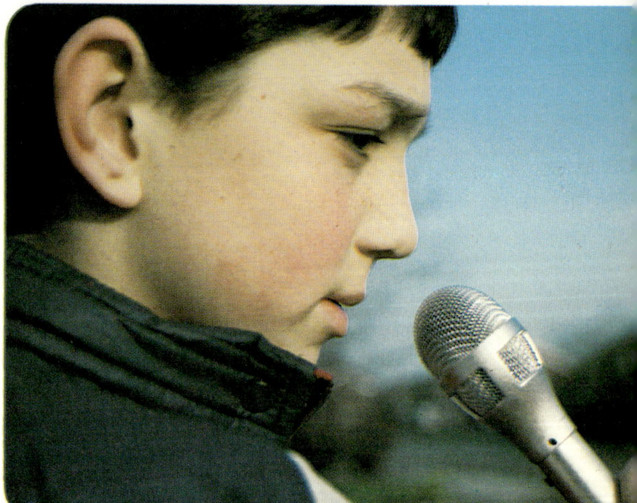

Make a megaphone from cardboard.

Test without the megaphone.

Test with the megaphone.

Test who can hear.

Test how well they can hear.

and Do

Read

Most sound comes through the air.

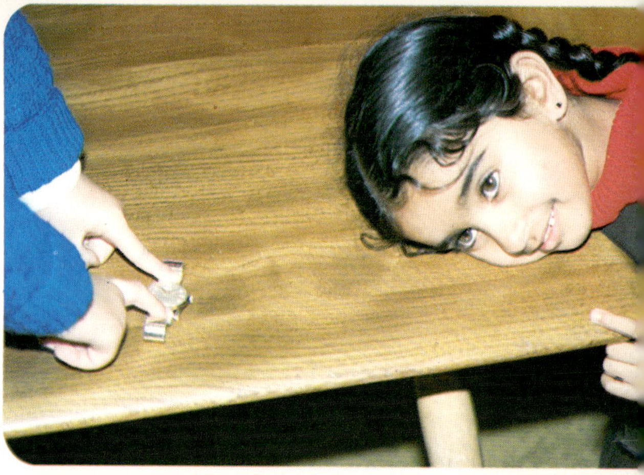

This girl can hear through wood.

This girl can hear through metal.

This girl can hear through brick.

They can hear the sounds.

Are they quiet or loud?

Listen through string.

Do a test like this.

Is the sound quiet?

Is the sound loud?

and Do

Read

This boy makes a loud shout.

He can hear an echo.

This boy makes a quiet whisper.

He can hear an echo.

.isten to echoes.

'ind places to hear loud echoes.

ıd places to hear quiet echoes.

Listen for echoes in an empty bucket.

and Do

Look at the pictures.
Find five things not the same.
Which make the sound loud?
Which make the sound quiet?

TO THE TEACHER

Most of the reading books suitable for very young children are stories and fantasies. There is much less reading material which relates directly to children doing things. This series aims to motivate children to read through practical activities and to begin simple science through their own reading.

It is important that the foundations for science education are laid now, as attitudes and interests are formed at this stage. These books encourage accurate observations and the use of all the senses to explore and compare. Basic concepts are dealt with through first-hand experience, which is the only way that real understanding can develop.

Realities of first-hand experiences are reinforced by photographic illustrations.

Concepts covered

The concepts of quiet and loud sounds are a development of the basic work covered in *Ears and Hearing*. Sound and its control are the major concepts introduced in this book.

Sound as a warning of imminent danger is an important concept that is emphasized within the text and the tests, as is the enhancement of sensual perception through careful listening. Children need this widening of experience of sound just as much as an extension of their other observational powers.

Children are encouraged to learn the skills of recording sounds and listening carefully to interpret them.

They gain the concept, through a wide variety of experiences, that sound is something moving and that distance determines volume.

They learn of several ways by which volume can be reduced or increased.

They find that sound travels differently through different materials.

They are introduced to the concept of the reflection of sound.

Possible extensions

Pages 2–3 Discuss other quiet and loud times and places. Identify which sounds are helpful and which disturbing and say whether they are loud or quiet.

Pages 4–5 Encourage the children to expand these examples to produce a sound quiz. E.g. which musical instrument? Whose voice? Which bird? What sort of vehicle?

Pages 6–7 Try listening to the radio or tape recorder in different places where the acoustics vary, e.g. bathroom or toilet, hall, sitting room, staff room.

Pages 8–9 Vary the height from which the pin is dropped and the surface on to which it is dropped. Note the sentence "Make the test fair". Vary only one thing at a time to ensure that only hearing is being tested.

Pages 10–11 Try coins of different sizes or other objects, such as paper clips, match boxes, nails.

Pages 12–13 Let the listener hear the sound at each mark then estimate the distance for random selections. Are some sounds easier than others to identify?

Pages 14–15 A contemporary extension would be to investigate the use of personal listening through earphones. Is this dangerous in some places? Repeat this test with earphones replacing the anorak. At what level can a

	danger signal, e.g. a bicycle bell, a car horn, still be heard?
Pages 16–17	Make megaphones different sizes.
Pages 18–19	Try passing sounds through a central heating system. Use different objects on the ends of the strings.
Pages 20–21	Visit places that are reputed to produce echoes.

Vocabulary and language analysis

This book has been carefully analyzed using two widely accepted readability formulae: the Fog Index and the Spache Readability Formula. Although it is written with children aged 6-8 in mind, the interest level will extend its use to children of 5+ who have reading ages within this range. Equally, many children of 9+ and 10+ who may be experiencing some reading difficulties will benefit from the challenge and increased motivation afforded by this series.

Words in this book regarded as unfamiliar or "hard" (Dale's List) for the Spache Test, together with those with three or more syllables used in calculating the Fog Index, are listed below:

bang, bedtime, brick, bucket, cannot, card, carpet, clang, clatter, coin, cracker, danger, different, echo, empty, fairground, glove, hood, knob, library, megaphone, metal, needle order, pan, pin, plate, playtime, radio, record, safe, shout, string, tape, tape recorder, test, tin, whisper.

Sixty-eight per cent of the words in this book are used in other of the first eight books in this series. Forty per cent are used in four or more. Sixteen per cent are used in all the first eight books.

Things you will need

tape recorder
blank tape
radio
pin
ruler
coin
rattle: small tin with stones or small nails
cardboard for megaphone
string
forks
metal bucket

Note

Page 22	Differences: ears covered; hat pulled down; clock on mat; mute in trombone; radio volume control altered.